EXERCISES IN
USING IDIOMS

Other titles of interest include

HEATON, J. B. and T. W. NOBLE
Using Idioms

LEE, W. R.
Study Dictionary of Social English

EXERCISES IN USING IDIOMS

J. B. Heaton

ENGLISH LANGUAGE TEACHING

PRENTICE HALL
New York London
Sydney Tokyo Toronto

First published 1987 by
Prentice Hall International (UK) Ltd
66 Wood Lane End, Hemel Hempstead,
Hertfordshire, HP2 4RG
 A division of
Simon & Schuster International Group

© 1987 J.B. Heaton

All rights reserved. No part of this publication may be
reproduced, stored in a retrieval system, or transmitted, in any
form or by any means, electronic, mechanical, photocopying,
recording or otherwise, without the prior permission of Prentice
Hall International (UK) Ltd. For permission within the United
States of America contact Prentice Hall Inc., Englewood Cliffs,
NJ 07632.

Printed and bound in Great Britain by
A. Wheaton & Co. Ltd, Exeter

Library of Congress Cataloging-in-Publication Data

Heaton, J. B. (John Brian)
 Exercises in using idioms.

 1. English language—Text-books for foreign speakers.
2. English language—Idioms. I. Title.
PE1128.H415 1987   428.2'4   87-1271
ISBN 0-13-294498-7

British Library Cataloguing in Publication Data

Heaton, J.B.:
 Exercises in using idioms.
 1. English language — Idioms 2. English language —
 Text-books for foreign speakers
 I Title
 428.2'4   PE1460
 ISBN 0-13-294498-7

1 2 3 4 5   91 90 89 88 87

CONTENTS

Introduction

Functional/Notional Groups of Exercises

1	Ability, inability, dullness	1
2	Effort	1
3	Knowledge, telling	2
4	Knowledge, ignorance	3
5	Sense, folly	3
6	Discovery, finding out	4
7	Certainty, doubt	4
8	Remembering, forgetting	5
9	Liking, disliking	5
10	Possibility, impossibility	6
11	Difficulty, ease	7
12	Disapproval, deceit, anger, calmness	7
13	Scorn, sarcasm	8
14	Suitable, unsuitable	8
15	Right, wrong	9
16	Criticism, praise	10
17	Important	10
18	Unimportant	11
19	Energetic, popular, ordinary, unique, successful	12
20	Persuasion, influence	12
21	Responsibility, independence	13
22	Authority, power	14
23	Honesty, deceit	14
24	Threatening, warning	15
25	Worry, anxiety	16
26	Anger, annoyance	16
27	Arguing, disagreeing	17
28	Determination	18
29	Enjoyment, pleasure, surprise, eating	18
30	Willingness, unwillingness	19
31	Bravery, fear	19
32	Surprise	19
33	Cost	20
34	Poor in quality, useful, useless	21
35	Failure, success	21
36	Wealth, poverty	22
37	Quantity, amount	23
38	Starting	23
39	Time	24
40	Similarities, differences	24
41	Ruin, harm	25
42	Age	26

43	Idioms from parts of the body	26
44	Idioms from colours	27
45	Idioms from animals	28
46	Idioms with make, give, put	29
47	Idioms from clothes	29
48	Miscellaneous	30
49	Miscellaneous	31
50	Miscellaneous	32
51	Miscellaneous	33
52	Miscellaneous	33
53	Miscellaneous	34
54	Miscellaneous	35
	Answer Key	36
	Index of Exercises	40

INTRODUCTION

EXERCISES IN USING IDIOMS provides practice in identifying common idioms in current use and is intended for students at intermediate and advanced levels. Maximum benefit can be obtained if the exercises in this book are attempted in conjunction with USING IDIOMS, but the book can also be used on its own, or with other dictionaries and reference books on idioms.

Like USING IDIOMS, this material is organised along functional/notional lines. For easy reference an index is provided, cross-referencing the exercises in this book with the relevant sections in USING IDIOMS. This is done to help students to see and learn related idioms in context. In addition, there are exercises on idioms grouped in other ways, e.g. colours, animals, parts of the body.

The exercises concentrate on recognition rather than production, since, in real life, students will chiefly be required to recognise and understand idioms without having to produce them. However, there are various types of exercises (multiple choice, matching, the completion of sentences and the production of suitable synonyms and antonyms) to increase motivation. Wherever possible, the exercises are presented in situational contexts, often within dialogues. Such contexts help the student to develop an awareness of how precise meanings and communicative values differ from one idiom to another within the same function or notion.

The exercises may be used in class under the guidance of the teacher or on a self-access basis by students working on their own. An answer key has been provided. Students may work steadily through EXERCISES IN USING IDIOMS or dip into the book, concentrating on individual sections as desired.

1 ABILITY, INABILITY, DULLNESS

Choose the most suitable words or phrases in the following conversations.

1. A: Miss Lee always knows what's happening in the office. She's extremely competent, isn't she?
   B: Yes, she's certainly **on** *the ball/the level/the mark/the line*.

2. A: Are you any good at decorating and fixing things in the house?
   B: I think so. I can **turn my** *head/arm/mind/hand* to most things.

3. A: Have you settled into your new job yet?
   B: I think I've **found my** *feet/toes/legs/hands*.

4. A: Why is Mr Lee giving private lessons? I thought he'd retired.
   B: He wants to **keep his** *mind to it/his hand in/a foot in the door/his head in the clouds*.

5. A: Can you drive this van?
   B: Yes, I've **got the** *feel/pull/hang/touch of it* now.

6. A: Simon Nelson doesn't seem very happy in his new job these days.
   B: No, I think he's **out of his** *depth/length/width/height*.

7. A: I don't think anyone understood much of Harry Thomson's lecture.
   B: No, it was certainly **above my** *face/hair/head/shoulders*.

8. A: Poor old Mr Thorpe is having a hard time checking to see who has paid and who hasn't.
   B: Yes, I know, but it's unfair to expect him to do this job at his age. I think he's *up to/down on/with/past* **it**.

9. A: It was ten minutes before Dave Hill saw the joke!
   B: He's very **slow on** *the ball/his fingertips/the uptake/his feet*.

10. A: I asked the old man on the bench for directions, but he just smiled at me.
    B: Oh, that's Old George. He's not quite **all** *in/there/that/out* these days.

2 EFFORT

Choose the most appropriate question or statement in each set to fit B's reply.

1. A: a. Do you think we'll manage to do it all in one day?
      b. Are a lot of people coming to the party?
      c. Is there much snow on the road?
   B: We should be able to if we all **get stuck in** straight away.

2. A: a. Why has Henry gone to the doctor's?
      b. How did Henry help you?
      c. Why did you say that Henry was lazy?
   B: He never **lifted a finger** to help me make supper for his friends last night.

3. A: a. Do you want me to stay or go?
        b. Shall we try to leave now?
        c. I don't think I could learn to ride a bicycle. I'd fall off.
    B: Come on, **have a go!**

4. A: a. I got 100% in the physics test at school yesterday.
        b. A lot of people have told me I'm growing very quickly.
        c. I'm not doing very well at all in physics, I don't think I'll pass the exam.
    B: You'll have to **pull your socks up** then, won't you.

5. A: a. I'm learning how to do Chinese brush painting.
        b. I've just bought another bicycle.
        c. I've decided to make a determined effort to pass the test.
    B: I'm glad you're **trying your hand at** something new.

6. A: a. I chose the flowers, but Mr Lee dug the garden and planted them.
        b. Mr Lee chose the flowers, but I dug the garden and planted them.
        c. I chose the flowers, dug the garden and planted them.
    B: I knew you'd get someone else to **do the donkey work.**

3 KNOWLEDGE, TELLING

Using the clues in the pictures, choose the correct idioms containing the verbs **know** *and* **talk** *to complete the conversations below.*

1. A: I don't think I'll ever be able to do this job.
    B: Don't worry. You'll soon **get to know** _____.

2. A: It's such a foggy night. Are you sure you want to drive there?
    B: Don't worry. I know the road **like** _____.

3. A: Do you think teachers really know when someone breaks the rules?
    B: Of course. Some of the teachers were pupils here, themselves. They **know** _____.

4. A: What did you think of the new manager?
   B: He's always **talking** _____. He doesn't seem to be able to have a conversation about anything besides his business.

5. A: Maria talks so much that it's hard to concentrate on what she's saying.
   B: I know. She **talks** _____.

4 KNOWLEDGE, IGNORANCE

Complete the following conversation with idioms containing the words in brackets.

A: You seem to (1)_____ **(way, around)**.
B: I've been here many times. I know this district (2)_____ **(back, hand)**.
A: By the way, have you ever met John Jameson?
B: I know the name, but I'm afraid I don't (3)_____ **(know, Adam)**. Why? Is he a friend of yours?
A: I've got (4)_____ **(nodding)** with him, but I don't know him well. It was he who gave me this map with these directions. It's absolutely useless. I can't make (5)_____ **(head, tail)** of it. Thank goodness I asked you.
B: Let me see the map for a moment. Oh dear. It's certainly (6)_____ **(Greek)** to me.
A: I really don't think he (7)_____ **(clue)** how to get to the station.
B. Just a minute. (8)_____ **(penny, drop)**. There's nothing wrong with the map at all.
A: No? I'm still (9)_____ **(dark)**. Show me!
B: Well, we're looking at the map upside down. Turn it round.
A: Ah, it's (10)_____ **(crystal)** now. He was quite right after all.

5 SENSE, FOLLY

*In the following dialogues, the idioms are **incorrect**. Replace each word in italics with the **correct** word. Note that the correct word is related in meaning to the word in italics.*

1. A: Alan Davidson is a very good businessman.
   B: Yes, he's certainly **got his head** *nailed* **on the right way**.

2. A: I wonder why Maria suddenly left a well-paid job to become a pop singer. Her voice is awful!
   B: She must be **out of her** *brain* to do such a stupid thing.

3. A: Will the company pay all my expenses?
   B: I think you'll be able to claim for anything **within** *explanation*.

4. A: Don't ever try taking drugs.
   B No, I shan't. It's **a mug's** *sport*!

5. A: Oh dear! I just swore at the boss.
   B: You ought to **have your** *mind* **examined** if you really did that.

6. A: Mrs Lee has decided to go back to her husband.
   B: I'm glad she's **come to her** *reason* at last.
7. A: Pauline is always sensible and realistic in her attitude to work.
   B: Yes, she always **keeps her** *toes* **planted firmly on the ground**.
8. A: I wonder why Harry does such silly things.
   B: I think he's got **a** *pin* **loose**.

6 DISCOVERY, FINDING OUT

Use the idioms in the list below to complete the conversation. (The idioms do NOT follow the order of the blanks in the conversation.) Put the verbs in the idioms in their correct form and make any other necessary changes.

catch someone red-handed   read between the lines
get wind of   pick someone's brains
straight from the horse's mouth   come to light

A: Do you mind if I _____ for a moment? It's about these accounts.
B: What's the matter with them?
A: It's something that _____ when I was studying them this morning. There's a mistake in them, and I think it may have been deliberate.
B: Who could have done that?
A: Tom Newling. He changed some figures in another set of accounts yesterday.
B: Are you sure?
A: Yes, I _____. Of course, he said he was just correcting them. I didn't know whether to believe him or not.
B: But he was highly recommended by his previous employers.
A: I know that, but I've looked again at one of his references.
B: And what did you find?
A: Well, _____, it almost looks as if his previous employers wanted to get rid of him. Perhaps they _____ what he was doing.
B: If I were you, I'd phone his previous employers and find out what happened _____.

7 CERTAINTY, DOUBT

Complete the conversation by putting the appropriate word in place of each blank.

A: Do you think we'll have to stand for the whole of the match?
B: We're (1) b_____ to get a seat if we get there before two.
A: Do you think we'll win?
B: It's **in the** (2) **b**_____. I don't think the other side will even score a goal.
A: Are you sure that John's got the tickets?
B: **There are no two** (3) **w**_____ about it. I saw him buy them.

A: We've got a good team, haven't we?
B: Yes — though Greystone Rovers are the (4) **h_____ favourites** to win the championship.
A: Have you heard whether Tim Hockney will be playing?
B: It's (5) **t_____ and go**. He hasn't fully recovered from last week's injury yet.
A: If we win, which team will we play against in the next round of the championship?
B: It's **anybody's** (6) **g_____**. We'll have to wait until the draw takes place next Friday to find out.
A: Where will the finals be played?
B: It's **in the** (7) **a_____** at present, but there's a chance they'll be played at Wembley.

8   REMEMBERING, FORGETTING

Choose the most suitable words or phrases in the following conversation.

A: Have you 'phoned Mr Watson yet?
B: Oh dear! I'm afraid it **slipped my** (1) *head/mind/brains/tongue* completely.
A: But you promised to phone him before seven! Honestly, you've got **a memory like a** (2) *sieve/tap/sponge/river*!
B: I **lost** (3) *path/memory/track/flight* of time since I started reading this detective story.
A: If you like detective stories, you should watch the film on TV tonight. It's quite good.
B: What's it called?
A: 'Murder on the ...'. Oh dear, it's **on the** (4) *cover/edge/tip/end* **of my** (5) *mind/tongue/memory/brain*.
B: 'Murder on the Asian Express'?
A: No, that's not it. But **it rings** (6) *an alarm/a chord/a bell/a phone*. It's something like that.
B: Oh, I know. 'Murder on the Orient Express'.
A: That's it. I've seen the film and I've read the book, too.
B: What's it about?
A: It's difficult to tell you. It's so long since I saw it. I've forgotten the details.
B: If you've seen the film and read the book I thought you'd know the story (7) **by** *brain/memory/heart/mind*!

9   LIKING, DISLIKING

Choose the most appropriate statement in each set to fit B's reply.

1. A: a. Linda and Susie hate each other, don't they?
        b. Linda and Susie are good friends.
        c. Linda and Susie are always fighting.
    B: Yes, they **hit it off** as soon as they met.

2. A: a. Ann can't do enough to please Tom.
        b. Ann hates Tom, doesn't she?
        c. Ann usually avoids Tom, doesn't she?
    B: Yes, she **thinks the world of** him.

3. A: a. Nigel's very keen on his new computer.
        b. Nigel's disappointed with his new computer.
        c. Nigel's worried about his new computer.
    B: Yes, he thinks it's the **best thing since sliced bread**.

4. A: a. The manager's fallen in love with Freda.
        b. The manager is always praising Freda.
        c. The manager always seems to be criticizing Freda.
    B: Yes, he's definitely **down on** her at the moment.

5. A: a. I'm crazy about classical music.
        b. I don't care much for classical music.
        c. I quite like listening to classical music.
    B: No, I **haven't got any time for** it, either.

10 POSSIBILITY, IMPOSSIBILITY

Read A's part of the following conversation. B's part is given below but the lines are not in the correct order. Put B's replies in the right order.

B's Part

And **pigs might fly**.

Yes, but I don't have **the ghost of a chance**.

No, it didn't, so at least I won't **stand to lose** anything.

Just **on the off-chance** that not many others would enter.

Do you really think I have **a sporting chance**?

A: Are you entering for the crossword competition?
B: 1._____
A: I wouldn't say that. I've never met anyone better at crosswords than you.
B: 2._____
A: Yes, I do. I bet you win.
B: 3._____
A: Why did you enter then?
B: 4._____
A: Did it cost anything to enter?
B: 5._____
A: I think you've got a good chance of winning. In fact, I'd say it's **on the cards** that you'll win.

11 DIFFICULTY, EASE

Complete the conversation by putting the most appropriate word in place of each blank.

A: I'm finding maths **hard** (1)_____ at college.
B: Is it more difficult than physics?
A: Yes, physics is a **piece of** (2)_____ compared with maths. There's (3)_____ **to it**.
B: I know what you mean. I found science **plain** (4)_____ at school, but I used to make **heavy** (5)_____ of every maths problem I was set.
A: Well, you certainly made **short** (6)_____ of the puzzle in my computer magazine yesterday.
B: I can do puzzles like those **standing on my** (7)_____. But not real maths. You know, at school we were just **thrown in at the deep** (8)_____ and told to get on with it. No explanation or anything — just difficult problems to solve.
A: It's surprising how many students have had to learn maths **the hard** (9)_____.
B: Yes, and there isn't much you can do about it when you're at school. You just have to (10)_____ **and bear it**.
A: And what's surprising is that most students succeed **against all the** (11)_____!

12 DISAPPROVAL, DECEIT, ANGER, CALMNESS

Use the idioms in the list below to replace the phrases in italics. Put the verbs in the idioms in their correct form and make any other necessary changes.

a snake in the grass
hit the ceiling
take it in (one's) stride
take a dim view
let fly at

get all steamed up
fly off the handle
take the heat out of the situation
do the dirty on
keep one's cool

A: Why did you (1) *lose your temper*?
B: I'm afraid I don't know. I (2) *got very upset* when Henry Anson said Ann Little was incompetent. He made me (3) *become extremely angry*.
A: You shouldn't have (4) *spoken so sharply to* him.
B: He's (5) *someone who can't be trusted*. He'd even (6) *be disloyal to* his best friend.
A: I also (7) *disapproved* of the way he spoke about Ann but at least I (8) *stayed calm*.
B: I'm sorry. I wish I could have (9) *accepted the situation without getting excited*.
A. Frank Hickson tried to (10) *calm things down* by changing the subject.

13 SCORN, SARCASM

Complete the conversations using the appropriate word (in its correct form) from the list below.

        turn   mickey   what   nose   deal   time   smack

1. A: Mrs Grant seems such a proud woman.
    B: Yes, she is. I wish she wouldn't **look down her** _____ at us all the time.

2. A: If you work hard, you'll be given a $10 rise at the end of the year.
    B: **Big** _____!

3. A: Sorry I'm late again.
    B: And so you should be! **I've no** _____ for people who are always late.

4. A: All my friends have received an invitation to Julie's party, but I haven't.
    B: That's a _____ **in the eye** for you, isn't it?

5. A: I want real jewellery — not imitation.
    B: But that necklace Harry gave you is lovely. You shouldn't _____ **your nose up** at it.

6. A: We're allowed to finish work an hour early on the day before the public holiday.
    B: So _____! That's the least the firm could do.

7. A: I think you look just like Michael Jackson.
    B: Are you **taking the** _____?
    A: No, I'm not. I'm serious.

14 SUITABLE, UNSUITABLE

Complete the following conversation with idioms containing the words in brackets.

A: Did you enjoy your holiday?
B: Great. It was just (1)_____ (**doctor**).
A: Where did you go?
B: Not far — only to Little Shoreham. We went camping. I swam every day, went climbing, played football, and even went cycling.
A: That would be just (2)_____ (**street**).
B: Yes, I was (3)_____ (**element**).
A: Perhaps it's just as well that your brother decided not to come. He'd have felt (4)_____ (**place**). He isn't really the outdoor type, is he?
B: No, he prefers reading to walking. In fact, he's more (5)_____ (**home**) in a library. It was lucky for him that he didn't come with us. He'd have felt like (6)_____ (**fish**).

15 RIGHT, WRONG

Using the clues in the pictures, choose the correct idioms to complete the short conversations below.

1. A: What's the capital of Papua New Guinea?
   B: Port Moresby.
   A: That's right. You're _____.

2. A: Did Harry Banks understand what I said?
   B: No, he didn't. He _____.

3. A: Is this the correct way of assembling the model?
   B: So far it is. You're _____.

4. A: This painting is awful. I don't care for it at all.
   B: I'm sorry you don't. Actually, I was the person who painted it.
   A: Oh dear. I've _____, haven't I?

5. A: The Inspector thinks Jackson is guilty. Do you agree?
   B: No. I think _____.

6. A: You've done very well on your first day in your new job.
   B: Thank you, sir.
   A: Yes, you've certainly started off _____.

7. A: Does your new employer know about your dismissal from your last job?
   B: No, he doesn't. So I'm starting off _____.

16 CRITICISM, PRAISE

Choose the most appropriate question or statement in each set to fit B's reply.

1. A: a. I'm quite interested in music, especially classical music.
      b. Although I say it myself, I'm very good at music.
      c. Do you think I'll be able to find a good music teacher?
   B: You like **blowing your own trumpet**, don't you?

2. A: a. The secretary and treasurer of the club were criticised.
      b. There was a lot of damage as a result of the accident.
      c. Several people were rescued by firemen and passers-by.
   B: Did anyone else **come under fire**?

3. A: a. Helen's an extremely good cook.
      b. Frank spends too much time drinking and going to nightclubs.
      c. Mr Simpson was praised for all his hard work.
   B: Well, that's a case of **the pot calling the kettle black**!

4. A: a. Steinway's new novel is extremely interesting.
      b. Steinway never takes much notice of the critics.
      c. Steinway is planning to write a new science-fiction novel.
   B: Yes, the critics have **praised it to the skies**.

5. A: a. I almost passed the examination.
      b. I'm taking an English test tomorrow.
      c. I managed to mend the puncture by myself.
   B: Well, I **give you full marks** for that.

6. A: a. Why did the supervisor criticise Ann?
      b. What did Ann do when the supervisor criticised her?
      c. How did the supervisor help Ann?
   B: She told her **where to get off**.

17 IMPORTANT

Complete the following sentences with idioms containing the words in brackets.

1. I decided to take the driving test at the last minute, but I was sure I wasn't ready for it. I practised for at least two hours every day for a fortnight. Oh, it was such hard work! Anyway, _____ (**long, short**) is that I passed!

2. Can you give me more details about the plan? I only know _____ (**bones**) at present.

3. The president of the company, the vice-president and the chief executive – in short, all _____ (**guns**) will visit our department tomorrow.

4. 'I don't want to move to a large town. I'm very happy being _____ (**fish, pond**),' said the chairman of the village council.

5. Several members of the committee are involved in the struggle for the powerful position of president. I wonder who'll emerge as _____ (**dog**).

6. The government gave the visiting politician _____ (**carpet**) even though he wasn't the president of his country.

7. 'I wonder if you know anyone _____ (**top**) who could use his influence to get me a job?' Belinda asked Mr Thompson.

8. Charles is now a _____ (**light**) in the local amateur dramatic society. In fact, he's just been elected secretary.

18 UNIMPORTANT

Using the clues in the pictures, choose the correct idioms to replace the words in italics in the sentences.

1. Now that you're no longer chairman of the club, you'll have to learn *to accept a less important position*.
2. It doesn't really matter whether Mary or Louise presents the prizes to the winners. It's all *a fuss about something unimportant*.
3. Although Edward *has only a small part in the plan*, he is nevertheless essential for its success.
4. The problem can soon be solved: don't *exaggerate its importance*.
5. Elspeth is tired of always *having a less important position than* her attractive and talented younger sister.

6. The part of Tokyo we've moved to is reasonably cheap, but as a place to live *it isn't specially interesting*.
7. Plans for a road between the island and the mainland have now been dropped, so the bridge is now *a matter which is no longer of any concern*.
8. It doesn't really matter whether I left at 4.15 or 4.20, does it? You're just *concentrating on unimportant details*.
9. There are times when Mr Edgehill *is not able to see what is really important because of his concern with unimportant details*.

19 ENERGETIC, POPULAR, ORDINARY, UNIQUE, SUCCESSFUL

Use the idioms in the list below to replace the phrases in italics.

a hit with
make or break it
run of the mill
make a go of it

go great guns
man in the street
middle of the road
out of this world

A: What do you think of the food in that restaurant?
B: Well, it's obvious they're not trying to cater for unusual or special tastes. I thought it was very (1) *average* really.
A: The first time I went I thought it was (2) *absolutely excellent* but I suppose it has become fairly (3) *ordinary* these days.
B: I suppose it's all right for the (4) *ordinary person* but not for anyone who is looking for something special.
A: Of course it may be (5) *very popular with* tourists. They're bound to like the general appearance of the place.
B: I expect the food will improve when the new owners take over the restaurant. Apparently they're determined to (6) *make it succeed*.
A: If they serve real Greek food, it'll (7) *be very successful*. There's a large Greek community around here.
B: Yes, but the actual quality of the cooking will (8) *be the most important factor in its success or failure*.

20 PERSUASION, INFLUENCE

Choose the most appropriate question or statement in each set to fit B's reply.
1. A: a. Do you know anyone musical?
   b. How on earth can I possibly get an interview?
   c. I'm not very strong. Can you help?
   B: I know someone who can **pull a few strings** for you.

2. A: a. Dave's done some excellent research.
   b. Dave's extremely honest in everything he does.
   c. Dave's a very good salesman.
   B: Well, I'd expect that, having spoken to him. He's certainly got **the gift of the gab**.

3. A: a. I wasn't very impressed by his arguments.
   b. I didn't influence many people.
   c. I hadn't a very interested audience.
   B: No, they **cut no ice with** me, either.

4. A: a. The salesman suggested I sold the car.
   b. There won't be any need to advertise this car at all. It's clearly superior to any other sports car currently available.
   c. Who persuaded you to buy the car?
   B: Yes. It **speaks for itself**.

5. A: a. Terry has a lot of influence over his girlfriend.
   b. Terry is always quarrelling with his girlfriend.
   c. Terry will do anything his girlfriend asks.
   B: Yes, she certainly **leads him by the nose**.

6. A: a. Only a few people will be influenced by Mr Lee.
   b. People will remember what Mr Lee has achieved for a long time.
   c. Mr Lee will soon be forgotten after he retires.
   B: I agree. He'll certainly **leave his mark on the company**.

21 RESPONSIBILITY, INDEPENDENCE

Complete the dialogues by putting the appropriate word in place of each blank.

1. A: You know that if someone in your department makes a mess of the job, you'll be blamed for it, don't you?
   B: Yes. I know that I'll have to **carry the** _____.

2. A: I refuse to wear a seat-belt.
   B: It'll be **on your own** _____ if you have an accident.

3. A: It wasn't my fault: it was Alice's.
   B: Stop **passing the** _____. You're the person who is responsible.

4. A: We're going ahead with the building of the new hotel.
   B: Well, I **wash my** _____ **of** the whole project: it'll be a disaster!

5. A: Mr Renfrew doesn't work very hard, does he?
   B: No, he doesn't seem to **pull his** _____.

6. A: I'll take care of these letters.
   B: No, Betty can do it. You've got **enough on your** _____ already.

7. A: I'll be back in half-an-hour.
   B: Don't leave me alone in the office **holding the** _____.

8. A: If your plan fails, we'll both be **in the** _____ **line**.
   B: Don't worry, you're more likely to be promoted.
9. A: Do you think the company will close this factory eventually?
   B: I don't know. Anyway, it's **no** _____ **off my nose**. I'm retiring this year.

22 AUTHORITY, POWER

Complete the conversation with the most appropriate idioms from the list below. Write the idiom in its correct form so that it fits in the context.

none of one's business
take a tough line
make one's presence felt
red tape
know which side one's bread is buttered on
send (someone) packing
keep an eye on (someone)
have no business
go by the book
at (someone's) beck and call

A: Ted Dixon's always laying down the law and ordering people about.
B: Yes, he likes to have people (1)_____.
A: Well, he's certainly (2)_____ since he took over as manager.
B: He's very fair, though. He always (3)_____.
A: Yes, but he (4)_____ to be rude to everyone.
B: I agree there. Why don't you say something?
A: I (5)_____. I don't want to lose my job. Why don't *you* complain?
B: It's (6)_____. I don't work in his department.
A: There's another thing I don't like. I wish there wasn't so much (7)_____.
B: The last time I complained about that, my boss (8)_____. They tend to (9)_____ with anyone they think is going to stir up trouble.
A: I know. I've got a feeling that they're (10)_____ just because I don't go around smiling all the time.

23 HONESTY, DECEIT

Choose the most suitable words or phrases in the following conversations.

1. A: You can't be serious.
   B: No, really, I'm **on the** *even/flat/smooth/level*.
2. A: You've got a good chance of winning a million dollars if you buy a new car and enter the competition.
   B: You must think I was **born** *today/yesterday/last week/last year*?
3. A: I feel I can trust Henry Dawson.
   B: Yes, he's **a man of his** *promise/word/letter/guarantee*.
4. A: Was there any attempt to bribe or threaten the jury?
   B: I can assure you that everything was **above** *the line/the top/board/the surface*.

5. A: These accounts don't add up properly.
    B: No, it looks like someone in the office has been **cooking** *the argument/oil/oven/books*.

6. A: Mr Shaw is very good at his business. He knows lots of people, and can bargain with them to get what he wants.
    B: He's very well known for his **wheeling and** *dealing/froing/goings/downs*.

7. A: I'll dismiss anyone who goes on strike.
    B: We'll be on strike from tomorrow all the same. We're going to *question/call/ask/pull* **your bluff**.

24 THREATENING, WARNING

Complete the conversations using the appropriate words from the list below.

| watch | play | screws | hold | pins |
| jump | step | steady | cut | ransom |

1. A: _____ **it out**. I'm tired of your practical jokes.
    B: I'm sorry. I won't play any more on you.

2. A: I won't recommend you for promotion if you don't do what I ask.
    B: Don't _____ **a pistol to my head**: I shan't be influenced.

3. A: If you do that to me again, I'll do the same to you. **Two can** _____ **at that game**.
    B: Sorry.

4. A: You're a silly old fool!
    B: _____ **it**! I'll sack you if you speak to me like that again!

5. A: You don't seem very happy.
    B: I'm not. **For two** _____, I'd resign now.

6. A: We'd better **watch our** _____ if we want to keep this job.
    B: Yes, nothing must go wrong this time.

7. A: Are you waiting for me to finish packing?
    B: Yes, and you'd better _____ **to it**! The bus goes in ten minutes!

8. A: We'll take our business away if you don't give us a better discount.
    B: Are you trying to **put the** _____ **on** me?

9. A: Are all the miners going on strike?
    B: Yes, but in my opinion it's wrong for a single group of workers to go on strike and so **hold the country to** _____.

10. A: I'm going to tell him what I think of him, right now!
    B: _____ **on**. If you just calm down, you'll find a better way of dealing with the situation.

25 WORRY, ANXIETY

Complete the conversations using the appropriate verbs in their correct form from the list below.

mind	get	make	have	worry
get	hold	cross	tear	clear

1. A: I must admit I was very anxious when I saw the plane land on one wheel.
   B: Yes, I was _____ **my breath** all the time.

2. A: You look very worried.
   B: Yes, I _____ **a few things on my mind** at the moment.

3. A: I'm sorry you were feeling annoyed. I hope you all understand now the reason for the company's change of policy.
   B: Yes, I think this meeting has _____ **the air** quite a bit.

4. A: I'm sure I've failed the maths exam.
   B: Well, it's all over now. It's no use _____ **in a stew** about it. You'll just have to hope for the best.

5. A: There's no need to _____ **your hair out**.
   B: You'd be furious if this had happened to you.

6. A: Sorry I'm late.
   B: You should have phoned. I've been _____ **to death**.

7. A: Mum, I don't like it here. Everyone's so boring!
   B: Hush, Jimmy! You'd better _____ **your P's and Q's** or no one will invite you again.

8. A: Oh dear. Are you sure I haven't upset Paul?
   B: I'm quite sure. Stop _____ **a mountain out of a molehill**.

9. A: Do you think it'll be difficult getting a return flight?
   B: I don't know. But we'll _____ **that bridge when we come to it**.

10. A: Would you like to tell me what happened?
    B: Yes. I'd like to talk about it and _____ **it out of my system**.

26 ANGER, ANNOYANCE

Complete the following conversations with idioms containing the words in brackets.

1. A: Why did Ann _____ (**fly/handle**)?
   B: I suppose she was very angry with me for being so scornful.

2. A: Didn't your brother _____ when you said that (**hit/ceiling**)?
   B: Yes, he did. He told me never to insult him in public again.

3. A: Why on earth did you _____ (blow/top)?
    B: Because Timothy forgot everything I told him.
4. A: Is there anything that ever gets _____ (blood/up)?
    B: Yes. Incompetence, laziness and sheer hypocrisy all make me very angry.
5. A: Why is Belinda _____ (do/nut)?
    B: Well, Henry's just broken her new hi-fi.
6. A: I know he was in a bad mood when I spoke to him. But he shouldn't have _____ (bite/head).
    B: No, I agree. It was wrong of him to speak like that to you. You'd done nothing to deserve it.
7. A: I hope I'm not _____ (tread/toes).
    B: Not at all. I don't mind in the least.
8. A: The noise of the pop music on his record-player _____ (get/nerves).
    B: Yes, I find it difficult to put up with the noise, too. It makes me very nervous.
9. A: Why don't you _____ (get/back)? You've been criticising me ever since I started this job.
    B: I'm sorry if I've annoyed you. I'm just trying to make sure the job is done properly.
10. A: All the seats had been sold. I could _____ (kick/myself) for not booking by phone.
    B: It really is a pity you didn't reserve seats.

27 ARGUING, DISAGREEING

Use the idioms in the list below to replace phrases or words in the conversation. The phrases are concerned with arguing *and* disagreeing *but are NOT shown in italics. However, the idioms listed follow the order of the phrases in the conversation. Put the verbs in the idioms in their correct form.*

at it	have it out
nothing of the kind	at loggerheads
of the same kind	talk at cross-purposes

A: Bill and his wife are always arguing about something.
B: That's completely untrue. They think the same way about almost everything.
A: Well, you should have heard them last night! Bill's wife really wanted to argue with him.
B: What were they arguing about?
A: Buying a dog. They were in complete disagreement.
B: But they already have a dog.
A: Bill and Jan Smart? No, they haven't!
B: Oh dear. I misunderstood. I'm talking about Bill Johnson and his wife — not Bill Smart!

17

28 DETERMINATION

Complete the conversations, using the appropriate words from the list below.

nothing   foot   heaven   stand
hook   heart   business   guns

1. A: Perhaps Mr Smart is right and I'm wrong after all.
   B: That's not true. **Stick to your** _____.
2. A: You're certainly very determined to get your old job back.
   B: Yes, I'd **move** _____ **and earth** to get it back.
3. A: Can I stay out until midnight, mum?
   B: No, you can't, Bill. I'm **putting my** _____ **down** this time.
4. A: You'll never rest until you get that watch, will you?
   B: No, I won't. I've **set my** _____ **on it**.
5. A: Why don't you forget about the incident? It's no use fighting against the government and the police.
   B: I shan't forget about it. We must **make a** _____ or there'll be no democracy.
6. A: She's determined to become chief executive.
   B: Yes, she's so ambitious she'll **stop at** _____.
7. A: Be careful. John Moore can be dangerous.
   B: I know. He'll try to get what he wants **by** _____ **or by crook**.
8. A: I'm determined to get the company back on its feet.
   B: Yes, I know you **mean** _____.

29 ENJOYMENT, PLEASURE, SURPRISE, EATING

Use the idioms in the list below to replace the phrases in italics.

on top of the world   bend over backwards
make a pig of myself   in stitches
let my hair down   the time of my life
took my breath away   couldn't believe my eyes

A: Did you enjoy yourself at the party?
B: Yes, I had (1) *a very enjoyable time*. What about you?
A: I really (2) *relaxed and enjoyed myself*.
B: I feel (3) *very happy indeed* now.
A. Yes, Mrs Hill (4) *made a real effort* to please us.
B: What did you think of Mr Hill's jokes?
A: Very funny. The last one had me (5) *in fits of laughter*.
B: And the food was excellent. I'm afraid I (6) *ate and drank far too much*.
A: I (7) *was really surprised* when I saw all the food.
B: Yes, it (8) *amazed me*, too.

30 WILLINGNESS, UNWILLINGNESS

Choose the most suitable words or phrases in the following conversation.

A: Why don't you play us a tune?
B: Not now. I'm not (1) *off my head/in the pink/in the mood.*
A: Oh, come on. You normally play (2) *at the drop of a hat/through your hat/eating your hat/taking your hat off.*
B: Well, I don't feel like it at the moment.
A: I'd (3) *lend an ear/get my skates on/give my right arm* to be able to play as well as you.
B: Would you be prepared to take lessons?
A: (4) *The sky's the limit/Like a shot/As often as not/Once in a blue moon.*
B: All right! (5) *No sooner said than done/Ten a penny/All in.* I know just the person!

31 BRAVERY, FEAR

Form idioms with the words in brackets to express the following sentences without changing their meaning.

1. I don't know how she was so bold as to do such a thing. (**nerve**)
2. Are you frightened now? (**cold feet**)
3. Well, don't be downhearted. (**chin**)
4. You'll terrify him if you do that. (**scare, life**)
5. I agree. She's been very unsettled and nervous all evening. (**cat, hot bricks**)
6. I'm sorry for making you very anxious. I didn't mean to. (**wind**)
7. Yes, those kinds of film terrify me. (**flesh, creep**)
8. I bet you felt very frightened and depressed. (**heart, boots**)
9. He kept calm and showed no sign of fear. (**turn, hair**)
10. Yes, I was. I felt very frightened. (**heart, mouth**)

32 SURPRISE

Complete the following conversations with idioms containing the words in brackets.

1. A: I heard you were going to appoint John Fife head of department.
   B: John Fife? That's ridiculous! _____ (**idea**)

2. A: Hello, Mr Smith. ... HELLO!
   B: Oh dear, I didn't see you standing behind me in the dark. _____ (**give, turn**)

3. A: The temperature fell last night to −20°C.
   B: Really? _____ (**say**)

4. A: Henry Travers won first prize.
   B: I'd never have guessed! _____ (turn up, books)

5. A: Look how easy it is to open the lock with this plastic card.
   B: Good gracious! _____ (live, learn)

6. A: How many cars were sold by the company last month?
   B: I'm sorry, I can't answer that without checking. _____ (catch, nap)

7. A: Did you have any idea that the factory was going to close?
   B: No. The news came _____ (bolt, blue)

8. A: What happened when the manager turned up at the party with his young secretary?
   B: You can guess. Their arrival _____ (raise, eyebrows)

9. A: David Clegg's just been made chairman.
   B: Well, _____! (I, blow)

10. A: What happened when Tina heard Bob had just got married?
    B: Actually, she was very calm. She _____ (bat, eyelid)

33 COST

Complete the conversations, using the most appropriate idioms from the list below.

        lost a packet   pretty penny
        for a song   ten a penny
        cut your coat   no object
        on a shoestring   paid the earth
        spoil the ship   daylight robbery

1. A: Did it cost a lot?
   B: Yes, **it cost a** _____.

2. A: Have you any idea how expensive it was?
   B: No, but you must have _____ for it.

3. A: I'm surprised he won't buy new machinery for the factory.
   B: Yes, he expects us to run his business _____.

4. A: How much did you pay for the watch?
   B: Not much. I bought it _____.

5. A: He charged me a hundred dollars for one lesson!
   B: Good gracious! That was _____!

6. A: We can't really afford to buy an expensive computer.
   B: Well, you'll just have to _____ **according to your cloth**.

7. A: Ted seems to throw his money about a lot.
   B: I know. Money seems to be _____ with him.
8. A: Are these electronic games expensive?
   B: Not really. They're _____ nowadays.
9. A: I lost two hundred dollars on the last race.
   B: I _____ on the same race.
10. A: Why don't we use cheap paper for the book?
    B: It seems a pity to _____ **for a ha'porth of tar**.

34 POOR IN QUALITY, USEFUL, USELESS

Complete the conversation with idioms formed from the words in the table.

a	in	loss
come	wild goose	good stead
a	you in	handy
stand	white	chase
a	dead	elephant

A: Don't throw that old piece of wood away.
B: Why not?
A: It may (1)_____. Is that a knife there?
B: Well, part of one — just the blade. Actually, it's an antique. I paid a lot for it, but it turned out to be (2)_____. It's worthless without its handle.
A: Yes, I see what you mean. It's (3)_____ as it is.
B: I've thought of going round the antique shops to see if I could find one for it.
A: You'd be wasting your time. It'd only be (4)_____.
B: Or maybe I could try to make a handle for it myself.
A: Well, you could always try. The experience will (5)_____ if you're interested in becoming a craftsman.

35 FAILURE, SUCCESS

In the following dialogues the idioms are incorrect. Replace the words in italics with the correct word. Note that the correct words are related in meaning to the words in italics.

1. A: Vincent Shaw has certainly **made his** *sign* **in the world**.
   B: I always thought he'd be very successful.
2. A: Ann Long's **got a lot** *moving* **for her**.
   B: Yes, she's intelligent, talented, beautiful and very lively.

3. A: Your party seems to **go with a** *roundabout*.
   B: Yes, everyone thoroughly enjoyed it.
4. A: I think Dave's **had his** *potatoes*.
   B: I think so too — in fact, I'm absolutely sure he'll lose his job.
5. A: Bill Dawson's **come down in the** *earth*.
   B: Yes, it's a shame he's been made redundant.
6. A: The People's Party is **a lost** *result*.
   B: I realise they can't win, but I'm voting for them on principle.
7. A: Our team **beat** Wanchai Wanderers *solid*, didn't they?
   B: Yes, I thought we'd win but I never guessed it would be by so much.
8. A: You're **fighting a losing** *war* trying to stop Harry gambling.
   B: I don't know. There's always a chance he'll reform.
9. A: Have you tried this cough mixture? It really **works** *marvels*.
   B: Yes, it's excellent.
10. A: You should have booked a seat yesterday. Now you've **missed the** *ship*.
    B: No, I haven't. It's not too late yet.

36 WEALTH, POVERTY

Complete B's part of the following conversation, in the correct order.

B's part
No, he isn't. I'm always **in the red**.
Well OK, if you pay me back. I'm not **made of money**.
Yes, he seems to **have an easy time of it**.
Again? I won't be able to **make ends meet** if I keep lending you money.
I wish I had one like it. He's obviously **struck it rich**.

A: Mr Mason is very well off.
B: 1. _____
A: He's living in the lap of luxury. Look at his new sports car.
B: 2. _____
A: Yes, he's got money to burn. He's not like you and me.
B: 3. _____
A: And I'm hard up, too. In fact, I don't have a bean at the moment. I don't know how I'll get home. Can I borrow something for the bus?
B: 4. _____
A: But all I need is £1. Just for tonight.
B: 5. _____

37 QUANTITY, AMOUNT

Complete the following conversation, using the most appropriate idioms from the list below.

across the board	the sky's the limit
chicken feed	hand over fist
a hundred and one	no end of
to the last man	thick and fast

A: Why did you apply for this job?
B: There are (1)_____ reasons. First, I think there's a lot of job satisfaction. Secondly, the firm has a good reputation. Thirdly, there seems to be (2)_____ opportunities. Fourthly, ...
A: Yes, quite. Unfortunately, the starting salary is low. Some people say it's (3)_____, but with your commission and bonuses you'll soon be making money (4)_____.
B: What about promotion?
A: Oh, promotion prospects come (5)_____.
B: Good. How senior could I eventually become?
A: (6)_____! You might even become Managing Director.
B: I heard rumours of a pay increase.
A: I'm sorry I forgot to tell you. There's going to be a 12% increase in pay (7)_____ — right from the Managing Director down to the humblest clerk. Now, have you got any more questions to ask me?
B: Yes, just one. Are you happy in your job?
A: Of course. Everyone in the firm is happy — (8)_____.

38 STARTING

Express the following sentences in the same way, using idioms formed with the words in brackets to replace the words in italics.

1. Who'd like to *begin* by asking the first question? (**ball, roll**)
2. Let's *start without wasting any more time* and finish decorating as soon as we can. (**crack**)
3. Tina *made a very good beginning* in the tennis championship by winning the first three games in the competition. (**get, fly**)
4. Isn't it time we *started the process* and obtained planning permission? (**put, wheels**)
5. Dave is very good at *starting to talk and getting people to relax* at a party. (**break, ice**)
6. Henrietta *started off badly* when she arrived ten minutes late on her first morning in her new job. (**get, foot**)
7. Mr Hickson's business went bankrupt and he had to *begin from nothing* once more. (**start, scratch**)
8. It's no good *starting before you're ready*. Wait until the building has been completely finished before you open the new shop. (**jump, gun**)

39 TIME

Choose A's most appropriate question or statement in each dialogue to fit B's reply.

1. A: a. I haven't seen Pat since last week.
      b. It's a long time since I saw Pat.
      c. I see Pat practically every day.
   B: Yes, I **haven't seen her for donkey's years**, either.

2. A: a. I'm sure Mr and Mrs Pemberton will be punctual.
      b. I think Mr and Mrs Pemberton will be late as usual.
      c. Mr and Mrs Pemberton will probably come early.
   B: Yes, they always arrive **on the dot**.

3. A: a. The plane crashed in the middle of a vast jungle.
      b. The plane crashed on the outskirts of a village.
      c. The plane crashed in the middle of a town.
   B: The survivors must have walked **for days on end** before getting help.

4. A: a. Mabel missed the train.
      b. Mabel arrived early for the train.
      c. Mabel only just caught the train.
   B: Yes, she **cut it fine**, didn't she?

5. A: a. I hear his new novel is doing as well as his others.
      b. I'm sure he'll never write another successful movel.
      c. I think his new novel really goes over the top.
   B: Yes, it was just **a flash in the pan**.

6. A: a. The rescuers reached the survivors just before they ran out of food and water.
      b. The rescuers reached the survivors, but it was too late.
      c. The rescuers reached the survivors only with great difficulty.
   B: Yes, They got there **in the nick of time**.

40 SIMILARITIES, DIFFERENCES

Choose A's most appropriate statement in each dialogue to fit B's reply.

1. A: a. This restaurant is **streets ahead of** the others around here.
      b. This restaurant **isn't a patch on** the others around here.
      c. This restaurant **has nothing on** the others around here.
   B: I agree: I think it's a lot better.

2. A: a. There's **little to choose between** our political views.
      b. My political ideas **go hand in hand with** yours, don't they?
      c. I'm afraid we are **poles apart** when it comes to politics.
   B: Yes, we'll never agree.

3. A: a. Look! Paul is **hand in hand** with Jonathan.
        b. Look! Paul and Jonathan are running **true to form**.
        c. Look! Paul and Jonathan are **neck and neck**.
    B: I didn't realise the race would be so close! I wonder who'll win.

4. A: a. Ted Law's **the spitting image of** Ronald Reagan.
        b. I've met Ronald Reagan, and Ted Law's **a chip off the old block**.
        c. There's **little to choose between** Ted Law and Ronald Reagan.
    B: Yes, he does look very much like him.

41 RUIN, HARM

Using the clues in the pictures, choose the correct idioms to replace the words in italics in the sentences.

1. I felt very depressed when the car broke down. It was *the one extra hardship that made it impossible to bear everything*.
2. Be careful and don't meddle in other people's affairs. You'll only *fail and be hurt*.
3. Harry's *lost his self-respect and become utterly worthless* since he was sacked.
4. The government knew that if the war continued, the country would be *brought close to defeat*.
5. Tim told Peter and Dave that if they *harmed Jerry in any way at all*, he'd tell their father.
6. You're only *causing yourself harm* by reducing all your prices.

7. What a pity! Their marriage is *breaking up* because he spends all his time gambling.
8. I'm *ruined and finished*: I tried everything to make the business a success but it's failed.

42 AGE

Complete the conversations, putting the appropriate word in place of each blank.

1. A: Come on and have a game of football with us.
   B: Oh, no. I'm _____ **it**.
   A: Who says you're too old!

2. A: Don't behave so stupidly. **Act your** _____.
   B: I'm sorry.

3. A: I think it's time to buy a new typewriter.
   B: Yes. The one we've got now has **seen better** _____.

4. A: How old is Mrs Smithers?
   B: She's over 70, but you couldn't tell. She's very **young at** _____. She even rides a motorcycle!

5. A: George always insists he's 62.
   B: That's not true. He's getting quite **long in the** _____. He must be 70 if he's a day.

6. A: Edward looks much older since his illness.
   B: Yes, he seemed quite young before, but now he certainly **looks his** _____.

7. A: I don't like any of the boys I've met so far.
   B: You can't be too fussy, Mary. If you don't get married soon, you'll find yourself **on the** _____.

8. A: The poor old woman's very ill, isn't she?
   B: Yes, I'm afraid she's got **one foot in the** _____.

9. A: Mr Jones is getting rather old for this kind of manual work.
   B: Yes, he is. It's time he was **put out to** _____.

10. A: The firm are appointing several young graduates.
    B: I know. They feel it's time there was some **new** _____ in the company.

43 IDIOMS FROM PARTS OF THE BODY

Complete the conversations, putting the name of the appropriate part of the body in place of each blank. (Put the word in its correct form: i.e. either singular or plural.)

1. A: Are you busy?
   B: Yes, I'm **up to my** _____ in work at the moment.

2. A: Did you pass the test?
   B: **By the skin of my** _____.

3. A: You ought to **put your** _____ **into your work**.
   B: I can't work much harder than I'm working at present.

4. A: Why did you apologise to Mrs Johnson when it wasn't your fault?
   B: Well, I wanted her to **save** _____. She was obviously very embarrassed and felt quite humiliated.

5. A: Do you mind if I **pick your** _____?
   B: Go ahead. What's your problem?

6. A: What's wrong with Vincent? He seems discontented and even aggressive.
   B: He's got a **chip on his** _____. He feels he should have been promoted instead of David.

7. A: Everyone should be equal. Don't you agree?
   B: No, I don't actually **see** _____ **to** _____ with you on this issue. I think your view is extremely naive.

8. A: The poor old man is obviously out of work.
   B: Yes, he looks very shabby and **down at** _____.

9. A: I do hope everything goes well at the interview.
   B: So do I. I'll **keep my** _____ **crossed** for you.

10. A: Why don't you **make a clean** _____ **of it**? Did you take the pen?
    B: Yes, I did — but I only borrowed it.

44 IDIOMS FROM COLOURS

Complete the conversations, putting the name of the appropriate colour from the list below in place of each blank.

green   black   red   white   blue

1. A: Oh dear! I've just got my bank statement for this month. I'm overdrawn by quite a lot.
   B: You oughtn't to spend so much money. You're always **in the** _____.

2. A: Was it really true that you'd just eaten?
   B: No, I'm afraid it was **a** _____ **lie**. I said that so Peter needn't invite me out to dinner.

3. A: Is your company going ahead with the construction of a cross-harbour tunnel?
   B: Yes, they've just got the _____ **light** from the government.

4. A: I think a lot of money was wasted on building the bridge. I know it's a beautiful bridge but will it ever be used much?
   B: I doubt it. It's another _____ **elephant** the government has encouraged.

5. A: What ever happened to Robert Dyson's youngest son?
    B: He was the _____ **sheep** of the family. He left school and ran away to join the navy when he was only seventeen.

6. A: Why did you get so angry?
    B: I always **see** _____ when people criticise my company without knowing anything at all about it.

7. A: Don't forget to sign this form in triplicate if you want a day's holiday.
    B: There are always so many rules here. I'm fed up with all this _____ **tape**.

8. A: Did you expect to win the competition?
    B: I'd absolutely no idea. It came out **of the** _____.

45 IDIOMS FROM ANIMALS

Complete the conversations, putting the name of the appropriate animal, bird or insect in place of each blank. (Put the word in its correct form: i.e. singular, plural, possessive, etc.)

1. A: What's the matter with Ted today? He can't sit still for one minute.
    B: I don't know, but he's **like a** _____ **on hot bricks**, isn't he?

2. A: Don't you believe Mr Nakamura?
    B: No, I don't. There's something wrong with his story. **I smell a** _____.

3. A: It **gets my** _____ to hear foreigners always complaining about our country.
    B: I agree. Why don't they leave if they don't like it here?

4. A: Mr Lawton thinks he's very important, doesn't he?
    B: Yes, he does. He's important only in our village. He's **a big** _____ **in a little pond**.

5. A: Don't trust Dave Talisman.
    B: Why not?
    A: He's a proper _____ **in the grass**.

6. A: Do you feel nervous?
    B: Yes, I've got _____ **in my stomach**.

7. A: Who are you getting to do **the** _____ **work**?
    B: Joe Bloggs. He doesn't mind looking up all these references.

8. A: Do you think Susan will take any notice of what you said?
    B: No, it'll be like **water off a** _____ **back**.

9. A: Did you know Thomas Wong's just won the first prize?
    B: Quiet! You've **let the** _____ **out of the bag**. The results haven't been announced officially yet.

10. A: How did you know about the principal's resignation?
    B: I got it **straight from the** _____ **mouth**.

46 IDIOMS WITH MAKE, GIVE, PUT

Using the clues in the pictures, choose the correct idioms containing the verbs **make, give** *and* **put** *to complete the sentences below.*

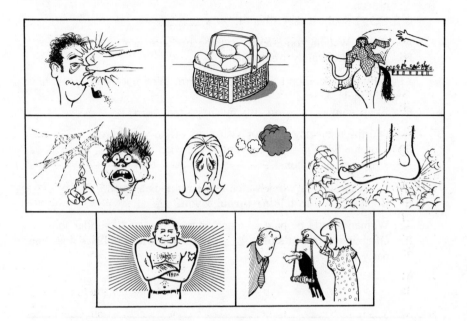

1. Mr Wright was **given** _____ when he wasn't even invited to the conference.
2. Why not invest small amounts of money in different companies? **Don't put** _____.
3. I hope 'Red Sails' wins. I've **put** _____.
4. The sight of the ghost **made** _____ and I began to tremble.
5. Esther **made** _____ when she heard the disappointing result.
6. Mr Lee **put** _____ and refused to allow his son to attend the pop-concert.
7. The army will **make** _____ **of him**.
8. Elsa **gave** Bill _____ and refused to see him.

47 IDIOMS FROM CLOTHES

Complete the dialogues, putting the appropriate item of clothing from the list below in place of each blank.

                 trousers   hat   shirt   socks
                 hat   shoestring   pants   hat

1. A: Please sir, I've forgotten to do my homework.
   B: You haven't done any homework for ages. It's time you **pulled you** _____ **up** and started to make an effort.

2. A: David Low plays the violin, paints and writes. He's a keen sportsman, too.
   B: I **take my** _____ **off to** him. He's very talented.

3. A: I'm sure the company will spend a lot of money on starting the new branch.
   B: Yes, I doubt if they'll run it **on a** _____.

4. A: Henry Waddington does everything his wife says.
   B: Yes, she certainly **wears the** _____.

5. A: Why on earth didn't you tell me before? Why not? You should have told me!
   B: **Keep your** _____ **on**. It's not important, is it?

6. A: Did the managing director visit your office yesterday?
   B: Yes, he did. I'm afraid he **caught me with my** _____ **down**. I was writing a letter home.

7. A: Everyone knows women aren't as ambitious as men.
   B: Rubbish. You're **talking through your** _____.

8. A: Women should be paid as much as men if they do similar jobs.
   B: Of course, but that's **old** _____ now. What new policies does your party have?

48 MISCELLANEOUS

Read the following articles from newspapers and choose the best headlines for each.

1.
DUTCH COURAGE

SINGING SOMEONE'S PRAISES

TAKING THE ROUGH WITH THE SMOOTH

WISHFUL THINKING

Philip Dunfold is 20 years old. He has not had a job since he left school four years ago. He has applied for over 100 jobs, but he can claim no qualification. None of his applications has been accepted.

When interviewed yesterday, however, he told reporters that he felt almost certain he would get a job as a clerk in some company or other, even though he cannot type.

2. **COMPUTERS TAKE A LOT OF BEATING**

COMPUTERS FIT THE BILL

COMPUTERS COME UNDER FIRE

COMPUTER GO HAYWIRE

Computers can cause serious stress, according to a recent report. Dr Vincent Ng, a senior psychiatrist at the Queen Elizabeth Hospital, emphasised in the report that such stress was no longer an individual problem but a much wider problem resulting from the increased sophistication of computer technology.
In addition, many leading educationalists are becoming concerned about the negative effect of computers on literacy and reading habits in general.

49 MISCELLANEOUS

Match each idiom on the left with its correct meaning on the right.

1. **a past master** (a) someone or something unable to survive without help
2. **a soft touch** (b) difficulties arising at the beginning
3. **a sporting chance** (c) highly likely to do something (eg. likely to win)
4. **a lame duck** (d) the favourite person

5. a hot favourite   (e) someone who can be easily blamed if anything goes wrong
6. a whizz kid   (f) an expert at something
7. the blue-eyed boy   (g) something completely useless
8. a fall guy   (h) a bright young person (successful in his/her job)
9. teething troubles   (i) a reasonable possibility
10. a dead loss   (j) someone from whom one can easily get money

Which idioms from this list best complete the following sentences?

1. David always does everything right: he's the teacher's _____.
2. The new company has now overcome its early _____ and is beginning to make a profit.
3. Helen is extremely kind and generous. Many people would say she is a _____, but I don't think she is easily fooled.
4. A: 'Alan Low is already an assistant manager and has helped to increase company profits by 150%.'
   B: 'Yes, he's certainly a _____.'

50 MISCELLANEOUS

The idioms in List A and List B are opposite in meaning. For each idiom in List A, find the opposite idiom in List B.

A

1. There are **no flies on** Robert.
2. The government's plans to cut inflation have come **under fire**.
3. Timothy is now **a big shot** in the company.
4. Alice is a girl **in a million**.
5. Billy is **in his element** now that he has the chance to play with your model railway.
6. Have you seen the new hotel? It's **out of this world**.

B

a. Avoid Harry Starr: he's **a nasty piece of work**.
b. The new restaurant is nothing special — just **run-of-the-mill**.
c. Poor David is **like a fish out of water** amongst all these experts.
d. Don't ask me — I'm just **a cog in the wheel**.
e. I'm afraid Mary's **as thick as two short planks**.
f. The new play was **praised to the skies**.

51 MISCELLANEOUS

Match each comment with the most appropriate picture. Write the number of the picture after each sentence.

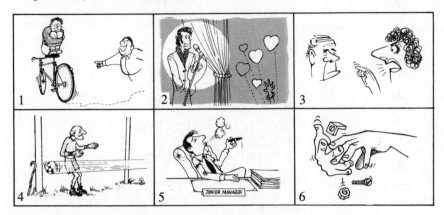

(a) He's a bit past it.
(b) I'm all fingers and thumbs this morning!
(c) He's got a screw loose!
(d) She's always laying down the law.
(e) He's a great hit tonight.
(f) You've certainly fallen on your feet.

52 MISCELLANEOUS

Read each of the following extracts from a newspaper and then choose the best headline.

1.
LOST CITY TURNS UP TRUMPS!

CUIDAD BLANCA STICKS ITS NECK OUT

ANCIENT CITY COMES TO LIGHT

OLD JUNGLE CITY PULLS ITS WEIGHT

A team of young explorers may have discovered the remains of a legendary lost city in the jungles of Honduras.

2. SHORTER WORKING
    HOURS IN JAPAN
    MAKE LIGHT WORK

    REDUCING WORKING
    HOURS IN JAPAN
    IS HARD-GOING

    SHORTER WORKING
    WEEK IN JAPAN IS
    JUST WHAT THE
    DOCTOR ORDERED

    LENGTH OF WORKING
    WEEK IN JAPAN IS
    KEEPING ITS END UP

    It has been some time since the call for a five-day week and shorter working hours in Japan was first heard. However, very little progress has so far been made.

53 MISCELLANEOUS

The idioms in List A and List B are opposite in meaning. For each idiom in List A, find the opposite idiom in List B.

A

1. Now that Mr Thornby controls the company, he can **call the tune**.
2. The junior manager **carried the can** for his secretary's mistake.
3. The mean old man **got his just deserts** when no one offered to help him.
4. William **blew his top** when he heard about the incident.
5. The old woman was **over the moon** when the mayor visited her.

B

a. If you don't **toe the line**, you'll be fired.
b. He **kept his cool** even though everyone else was shouting and raving.
c. Tom was **down in the dumps** as a result of his failure when I saw him.
d. Hannah **gets away with blue murder**. She's untidy and forgetful but no one ever complains.
e. The manager tried to **pass the buck** to his two assistants, but they refused to accept responsibility for the error.

54 MISCELLANEOUS

Using the clues in the pictures, choose the correct idioms to complete the sentences below.

1. David was _____ of the family. He was idle, deceitful, and he spent all his time gambling and drinking.
2. I felt like _____ at the party. Everyone was much older and a lot richer than I was.
3. Anyone with an ounce of sense can solve this problem. It's _____.
4. Petra's a real _____ and is always running around doing something.
5. Toni's got _____ about dieting: she's always most careful about everything she eats.
6. Unfortunately, the writer's early success was just _____. His subsequent novels were never as good as his first novel.
7. Although Helen and Sarah are close friends, they're as different from each other as _____.
8. The small patrol soon realised they were _____ and could easily be attacked from all sides.
9. Mary Hill's really _____: sales have trebled since she was appointed sales manager.

ANSWER KEY

Exercise 1
1. the ball
2. hand
3. feet
4. his hand in
5. feel
6. depth
7. head
8. past
9. the uptake
10. there

Exercise 2
1. a
2. c
3. c
4. c
5. a
6. a

Exercise 3
1. the ropes
2. the back of my hand
3. the score
4. shop
5. nineteen to the dozen

Exercise 4
1. know your way around
2. like the back of my hand
3. know him from Adam
4. a nodding acquaintance
5. head or tail
6. all Greek to me
7. has a clue
8. The penny's (just) dropped
9. in the dark
10. crystal clear

Exercise 5
1. screwed
2. mind
3. reason
4. game
5. head
6. senses
7. feet
8. screw

Exercise 6
1. pick your brains
2. came to light
3. caught him red-handed
4. reading between the lines
5. got wind of
6. straight from the horse's mouth

Exercise 7
1. bound
2. bag
3. ways
4. hot
5. touch
6. guess
7. air

Exercise 8
1. mind
2. sieve
3. track
4. tip
5. tongue
6. a bell
7. heart

Exercise 9
1. b
2. a
3. a
4. c
5. b

Exercise 10
1. Yes, but I don't have the ghost of a chance.
2. Do you really think I have a sporting chance?
3. And pigs might fly.
4. Just on the off-chance that not many others would enter.
5. No, there wasn't, and so at least I won't stand to lose anything.

Exercise 11
1. going
2. cake
3. nothing
4. sailing
5. weather
6. work
7. head
8. end
9. way
10. grin
11. odds

Exercise 12
1. fly off the handle/hit the ceiling
2. get all steamed up
3. hit the ceiling/fly off the handle
4. let fly at
5. a snake in the grass
6. do the dirty on
7. took a dim view
8. kept my cool
9. taken it in my stride
10. take the heat out of the situation

Exercise 13
1. nose
2. deal
3. time
4. smack
5. turn
6. what
7. mickey

Exercise 14
1. what the doctor ordered
2. up your street
3. in my element
4. out of place
5. at home
6. a fish out of water

Exercise 15
1. spot on
2. got hold of the wrong end of the stick
3. on the right track
4. dropped a brick
5. he's barking up the wrong tree.
6. on the right foot
7. with a clean slate

Exercise 16
1. b
2. a
3. b
4. a
5. c
6. b

Exercise 17
1. the long and short of it
2. the bare bones
3. the big guns
4. a big fish in a small pond
5. top dog
6. the red carpet (treatment)
7. at the top
8. leading light

Exercise 18
1. take a back seat
2. storm in a teacup
3. is only a cog in the wheel
4. make a mountain out of a molehill
5. playing second fiddle to
6. it's nothing to write home about
7. a dead duck
8. splitting hairs
9. can't see the wood for the trees

Exercise 19
1. middle of the road
2. out of the world
3. run of the mill
4. man in the street
5. a hit with
6. make a go of it
7. go great guns
8. make or break it

Exercise 20
1. b
2. c
3. a
4. b
5. c
6. b

Exercise 21
1. can
2. head
3. buck
4. hands
5. weight
6. plate
7. fort
8. firing
9. skin

Exercise 22
1. at his beck and call
2. made his presence felt
3. goes by the book
4. has no business
5. know which side my bread is buttered on
6. none of my business
7. red tape
8. sent me packing
9. take a tough line
10. keeping an eye on me

Exercise 23
1. level
2. yesterday
3. word
4. board
5. books
6. dealing
7. call

Exercise 24
1. cut
2. hold
3. play
4. watch
5. pins
6. step
7. jump
8. screws
9. ransom
10. steady

Exercise 25
1. held
2. have
3. cleared
4. getting
5. tear
6. worried
7. mind
8. making
9. cross
10. get

Exercise 26
1. fly off the handle
2. hit the ceiling
3. blow your top
4. your blood up
5. doing her nut
6. bitten my head off
7. treading on your toes
8. is getting/gets on my nerves
9. get off my back
10. kicked myself

Exercise 27
A: Bill and his wife are always at it.
B: Nothing of the kind. They are of the same mind about almost everything.
A: Well, you should have heard them last night. Bill's wife obviously wanted to have it out with him.
B: What were they arguing about?
A: Buying a dog. They were at loggerheads about it.
A: But they've already got a dog.
B: Bill and Jane Smart? No, they haven't!
B: Oh dear. I'm/We're talking at cross-purposes. I'm talking about Bill Johnson and his wife — not Bill Smart!

Exercise 28
1. guns
2. heaven
3. foot
4. heart
5. stand
6. nothing
7. hook
8. business

Exercise 29
1. the time of my life
2. let my hair down
   (or had the time of my life)
3. on top of the world
4. bent over backwards
5. in stitches

6. made a pig of myself
7. couldn't believe my eyes
8. took my breath away

Exercise 30
1. in the mood
2. at the drop of a hat
3. give my right arm
4. like a shot
5. no sooner said than done

Exercise 31
1. ... How she had the nerve to do such a thing
2. Have you (got) cold feet now?
3. Well, keep your chin up.
4. You'll scare the life out of him if ...
5. ... She's been like a cat on hot bricks all evening.
6. I'm sorry for putting the wind up you ...
7. Yes, those kinds of films make my flesh creep.
8. I bet your heart was in your boots.
9. He (kept calm and) didn't turn a hair.
10. ... My heart was in my mouth.

Exercise 32
1. The (very) idea.
2. You gave me (quite) a turn.
3. You don't say!
4. That's a turn up for the books.
5. You/We live and learn
6. You've caught me napping
7. like a bolt out of/from the blue
8. raised several/quite a few eyebrows
9. I'm blowed/I'll be blowed
10. She didn't bat an eyelid

Exercise 33
1. pretty penny
2. paid the earth
3. on a shoestring
4. for a song
5. daylight robbery
6. cut your coat
7. no object
8. ten a penny
9. lost a packet
10. spoil the ship

Exercise 34
1. come in handy
2. a white elephant
3. a dead loss
4. a wild goose chase
5. stand you in good stead

Exercise 35
1. mark
2. going
3. swing
4. chips
5. world
6. cause
7. hollow
8. battle
9. wonders
10. boat

Exercise 36
1. Yes, he seems to have an easy time of it.
2. I wish I had one like it. He's obviously struck it rich.
3. No, he isn't. I'm always in the red.
4. Again? I can't make ends meet if I'm always lending you money.
5. Well, OK, if you pay me back. I'm not made of money.

Exercise 37
1. No end of/a hundred and one
2. a hundred and one/no end of
3. chicken feed
4. hand over fist
5. thick and fast
6. The sky's the limit.
7. across the board
8. to the last man

Exercise 38
1. start the ball rolling
2. get cracking
3. got off to a flying start
4. set the wheels in motion
5. breaking the ice
6. got off on the wrong foot
7. start from scratch
8. jumping the gun

Exercise 39
1. b
2. a
3. b
4. c
5. b
6. a

Exercise 40
1. a
2. c
3. c
4. a

Exercise 41
1. the last straw
2. get your fingers burnt
3. gone to the dogs
4. brought to its knees
5. laid a finger on Daisy
6. cutting your own throat
7. on the rocks
8. all washed up

Exercise 42
1. past
2. age
3. days
4. heart
5. tooth
6. age
7. shelf
8. grave
9. grass
10. blood

Exercise 43
1. eyes
2. teeth
3. back
4. face
5. brains
6. shoulder
7. eye
8. heel
9. fingers
10. breast

Exercise 44
1. red
2. white
3. green
4. white
5. black
6. red
7. red
8. blue

Exercise 45
1. cat
2. rat
3. goat
4. fish
5. snake
6. butterflies
7. donkey
8. duck's
9. cat
10. horse's

Exercise 46
1. a smack in the eye
2. all your eggs in one/the same basket
3. my shirt on it
4. my hair stand on end
5. a long face
6. his foot down
7. a man
8. the bird

Exercise 47
1. socks
2. hat
3. shoestring
4. trousers/pants
5. shirt
6. pants/trousers
7. hat
8. hat

Exercise 48
1. Wishful thinking
2. Computers come under fire

Exercise 49
1. f
2. j
3. i
4. a
5. c
6. h
7. d
8. e
9. b
10. g

1. blue-eyed boy
2. teething troubles
3. soft touch
4. whizz kid

Exercise 50
1. e
2. f
3. d
4. a
5. c
6. b

Exercise 51
Picture 1: He's got a screw loose!
Picture 2: He's a great hit tonight.
Picture 3: She's always laying down the law.
Picture 4: He's a bit past it!
Picture 5: You've certainly fallen on your feet.
Picture 6: I'm all fingers and thumbs this morning!

Exercise 52
1. Ancient city comes to light
2. Reducing working hours in Japan is hard-going

Exercise 53
1. a
2. e
3. d
4. b
5. c

Exercise 54
1. the black sheep
2. a fish out of water
3. a piece of cake
4. ball of fire
5. a bee in her bonnet
6. a flash in the pan
7. chalk and cheese
8. sitting ducks
9. on the ball

INDEX OF EXERCISES
(Containing references to the appropriate sections in USING IDIOMS)

Function, notion, attitude, topic, etc.	Section in this book	Section in Using Idioms	Function, notion, attitude, topic, etc.	Section in this book	Section in Using Idioms
Ability	1	1	Ordinary	19	52
Age	42	108	Parts of the body	43	—
Amount	37	134	Persuasion	20	63
Anger	12, 26	76	Pleasure	29	80
Animals	45	—	Poor in quality	34	44
Annoyance	26	76	Popular	19	31
Anxiety	25	74	Possibility	10	18
Arguing	27	98	Poverty	36	105
Authority	22	60	Power	22	60
Bravery	31	86	Praise	16	40
Calmness	12	78	*Put*	46	—
Certainty	7	20	Quantity	37	134
Clothes	47	—	Remembering	8	28
Colours	44	—	Responsibility	21	61
Cost	33	103	Right	15	41
Criticism	16	39	Ruin	41	112
Deceit	12, 23	59	Sarcasm	13	35
Determination	28	84	Scorn	13	35
Differences	40	136	Sense	5	16
Difficulty	11	7	Similarities	40	135
Disagreeing	27	100	Starting	38	127
Disapproval	12	33	Success	35	114
Discovery	6	13	Successful	19	114
Disliking	9	32	Suitable	14	48
Doubt	7	21	Surprise	29, 32	94
Drinking	27	101	Telling	3	96
Dullness	1	4	Threatening	24	65
Ease	11	8	Time	39	129
Eating	29	101	Unimportant	18	51
Effort	2	5	Unique	19	53
Energetic	19	6	Unsuitable	14	49
Enjoyment	29	79	Unwillingness	30	89
Failure	35	113	Useful	34	46
Fear	31	87	Useless	34	47
Finding out	6	13	Warning	24	65
Folly	5	17	Wealth	36	104
Forgetting	8	29	Willingness	30	88
Give	46	—	Worry	25	74
Harm	41	112	Wrong	15	42
Honesty	23	58			
Ignorance	4	10			
Important	17	50			
Impossibility	10	19			
Inability	1	2			
Independence	21	71			
Influence	20	63			
Knowledge	3, 4	9			
Liking	9	30			
Make	46	—			
Miscellaneous	48, 49, 50, 51, 52, 53, 54	—			